Contents

Welcome!

Those of you up in the northern hemisphere might have Norway and Iceland, but New Zealand's hectic tramping trails, 3,000m+ mountain peaks, epic geothermal wonders, and top-notch lakes to kayak are well worth the long-haul flight. Be on the lookout for the elusive Kiwi bird, and always be sure to leave no trace – New Zealand's pristine ecosystems are outstanding for one reason: the locals know how to explore sustainably.

Whangarei
Auckland
Rotorua
Taupo
Nelson
Wellington
Christchurch
Wanaka
Queenstown
Dunedin
Invercargill
Stewart Island

Our Insiders' Picks of the Top 10 Experiences in New Zealand

Explore Fiordland beyond Milford Sound

Sure, the gateway to Milford Sound looks great from the rocky foreshore, but imagine kayaking beneath tumbling waterfalls and finding seals perched on boulders deep inside the channels of the sounds.

Don't just take a day-cruise. Instead, if you've got a hire car, stop off along Milford Road to check out these less-crowded highlights. Stop to take in Lake Marian after a three-hour return, 1.5mi (2.4km) hike, park up at The Divide for a walk up Key Summit (three hours, 2.11mi/3.4km), or take a short trip to The Chasm (20min, 400m) to see the narrow gorge with the Cleddau River thundering through.

Better yet, if you've got more time (and a little more budget), head to Doubtful Sound. This part of Fiordland is much larger than Milford, so you'll need at least a few days to make the most of the region.

Seals at Milford Sound

Kiwi birds and kayaks on Stewart Island

If you're looking for a real sense of isolation, look no further (well, it's pretty far) than Stewart Island, tucked away at the southernmost end of the country.

This is an ideal destination for nature lovers and adventure seekers, and one of the best places to see the elusive Kiwi bird. Here, the endangered national icon outnumbers human residents (400 humans to roughly 13,000 Kiwi birds).

At dusk, kayak along Stewart Island's peaceful bays. The island's southerly position means late, lingering sunsets and sunrises in summer. Be sure to visit around December–February.

Experience geo-thermal wonders at Lake Taupo

While Rotorua is considered New Zealand's geothermal capital, smaller Taupo is worth a visit if you want to avoid crowds. Situated on Lake Taupo – the crater of a super volcano – the whole town looks toward the snow-capped peaks of three active volcanoes: Tongariro, Ruapehu, and Ngauruhoe.

Dip your toes into the layers of volcanic pumice on Lake Taupo's shoreline and feel hot water seeping below your feet. Or, head to the hot waterfall of Otumuheke Stream at Spa Park, where locals submerge themselves with a cold beer in hand, watching the swirling Waikato River. The stream mixes with cool river water, so there's a temperature to suit everyone.

Take on the Tongariro Alpine Crossing

An adventure on the North Island would be incomplete without hiking this famous alpine crossing. In just one day, you'll weave your way by three volcanoes: Tongariro, Ruapehu, and Ngauruhoe – which you might recognize from *The Lord of the Rings*.

Challenges on the 12.5mi (20km) hike include the 'devil's staircase' and slippery scree slopes, but you'll be rewarded with incredible turquoise sulphur lakes and a volcanic moonscape. Keep in mind (like everywhere else in New Zealand) the weather can be temperamental, so come prepared with waterproof clothing and layers.

Visit sacred Cape Reinga

Get your own vehicle and camping

Weather in Fiordland

It can snow here any month of the year, and can rain a meter in a day. Fiordland is, essentially, a rainforest. This is good in terms of the sheer volume of waterfalls, but it means you need to embrace the idea of getting wet. You should also have alternative plans in case access to Milford or Doubtful is closed, which happens occasionally at times of high rain or avalanche risk.

Tongariro Alpine Crossing

gear to see Northland, and give yourself at least four or five days to take it all in. Catch a sunset from Cape Reinga, where the ancient pohutukawa tree stands, and – so the legend goes – spirits take the leap to go back to their ancestral home.

It's a six-hour drive north of Auckland on route nr1, so be sure to stop in at remote bays, like Spirits Bay and Matai Bay, along the way.

On your way back, go sandboarding at Te Paki Sand Dunes. Hold on tight to your boogie board, because you're not stopping until you hit the bottom.

Unwind at Piha and the Waitakere Ranges

West of Auckland lies the Waitakere Ranges (the Waitaks, in local speak). Start your adventure with a drive to Piha (pronounced Pee-ha), arguably New Zealand's most beautiful beach. Don't let any weather put you off. If it's sunny, great. If not, even better. Piha is a driftwood-strewn, black-sand beach with thundering surf – it's best in wet, windy weather.

Take the Kitekite track to Kitekite Falls. The vegetation in this area is beautiful, studded with nikau palms, fern fronds, and native birds, and the falls at the end of the track are worth the walk.

Escape the crowds at one of the stunning but seldom-visited beaches nearby – Anawhata is the best of the bunch. It's a steep (but well-maintained) walk from the carpark down to the beach, and you'll likely be the only people there.

> " A short drive past the bright turquoise waters of Lake Dunstan brings you to Lake Wanaka and Lake Hawea.

Lake Wanaka

Milly McGrath

Lake Wanaka and Hawea

A short drive past the bright turquoise waters of Lake Dunstan brings you to Lake Wanaka and Lake Hawea. Here, you'll find yourself at the edge of the stunning, snow-capped Southern Alps.

Although Wanaka is a must-stop for many tourists on their journey through the South Island, if you look beyond 'that Wanaka tree' and Roy's Peak, the surrounding National Parks and Conservation Areas can easily pull you away from queues of photographers and tourists. Some quieter alternatives to Roy's Peak are Isthmus Peak and Breast Hill, both of which have equally bewildering views.

Hike to the base of New Zealand's highest mountain

One of the easiest and best day-hikes would have to be the Hooker Valley Track. Winding its way from White Horse Hill campsite to the glacial lake at the foot of Mount Cook, you'll be surrounded by happy hikers as you walk along high suspension bridges and wooden walkways.

Aim to start the hike an hour

Approaching Lindis Pass

If the South Island is your destination, be sure to try Gillespies Pass, the Kepler Track, or the Routeburn. If it's the Noth Island you're tramping, check out Tongariro Alpine Crossing, Rangitoto Summit, and the Putangirua Pinnacles.

Hire a campervan to make the most of it

Getting a hire car is a great way to see the sights yourself. But, spending a little extra to hire a campervan (once you consider the money saved on accommodation) makes complete sense. Campsites aren't expensive, especially if you aim to go for the free DOCs sites – despite limited facilities, they've got the ultimate views.

Don't just follow the well-known West Coast on the South Island or Auckland to Wellington, ask around when you arrive to get advice from those that know best – the locals. They'll deliver when it comes to secret coves and quiet lake-side campsites.

before sunrise or sunset and you'll be rewarded with fairy-floss colored skies and less crowds. Pack a snack to enjoy while watching the icebergs bobbing around the lake (unless you're there in winter, when it's totally frozen over).

Hut-to-hut hikes and DOCs campsites

New Zealand's Department of Conservation (DOC) manages over 200 campsites and over 950 huts. Book your sites in advance if you're traveling during peak season (October–April), and know the huts vary in amenities, but most have a big bunk bed and a wood-burning stove.

To really get into the tramping spirit, lace up your hiking boots, pack clothing to suit all weather conditions (New Zealand's weather is temperamental), and study the trails you plan to tackle.

Preparing for Hut-to-Hut Tramping

If you're heading out overnight on foot, you're not hiking: you're tramping. New Zealand has an amazing network of tramping huts, all maintained by the loveable Department of Conservation (DOC). Huts have bunks with mattresses and a water supply, but no food, cooking equipment, or rubbish bins.

Visit your local DOC visitors' center before you head out on a tramp. The staff have the latest updates on track conditions, weather forecasts, and numbers of other trampers in the area. You can buy maps, and the they can give you a run-down on your route.

This is also where you hire personal location beacons – essential if you're heading off by yourself, and a very good idea if you're heading off in a group. If you have a major emergency, you can set off your locator beacon, and search and rescue will come find you. Chances are you'll never use it, but it's the best safety net you'll get.

North vs South Island

There's a stereotype that the North Island is more cosmopolitan and the South Island more rural – but the reality is you can find plenty of farmland and cityscape on both. If you have enough time, check them both out.

Where to go for culture and sight-seeing

The North Island is the best destination for culture and sight-seeing. Visit the capital city, Wellington, and stop by the Te Papa museum to get a quick run-down on New Zealand's history (it's free!).

Visit the Waitangi Treaty Grounds in the Bay of Islands, where the Maori and the British signed a treaty. You'll get a guided tour and be welcomed onto a *marae* (a meeting place) with a *powhiri* (a welcoming dance).

Stay in nearby Russell or Paihia for stunning views of the coastline and one of the best jumping-off points to see dolphins in the wild.

Temple Basin, Arthur's Pass

Leader de Brauwer

> " Sure, you can bungee jump off Auckland's Harbor Bridge, but if you're a real adventure junkie, go to Queenstown.

Where to go for adventure and road-trips

Sure, you can bungee jump off Auckland's Harbor Bridge, but if you're a real adventure junkie, go to Queenstown. It's the best place in New Zealand for thrill-seekers and has beautiful scenery, with picturesque mountains surrounding a glassy lake.

During winter, the slopes are popular, but there's plenty to do year-round. Go bungee jumping, quad-biking, hiking, sky-diving, or river-boarding – you name it, Queenstown's got it.

If you've got a car, take the scenic route from Queenstown to Wanaka, through Arrowtown and Cardrona. Another great option is to rent a campervan in Nelson and drive along the coast to Collingwood, seeing the Abel Tasman National Park along the way.

Waitangi

Climate and Weather

New Zealand's incredible scenery, friendly locals, and endless choices for adventure make it a top destination year-round, but when should you go?

Best times to visit

Keep in mind, New Zealand is almost as close to Antarctica as it is to those sunny islands dotted around the Pacific Ocean. Where and when to visit depends on how long you have, whether you're seeking adventure, culture, or sightseeing, and if it's snowboarding or warm-weather hiking you're after.

Seasons

There are huge differences in temperature between Cape Reinga at the top of the North Island, and Invercargill at the bottom of the South Island.

Winters (June – August) are cold and rainy in the north, and near-freezing in the south. The houses in New Zealand

Remarkables, Queenstown

Sam Grimmer

Mt Fyffe Hut

> Try to visit during one of the shoulder seasons, Spring or Autumn when there should be less tourists, lower prices less extreme temperatures.

are also notoriously poorly-insulated. Be sure to bring proper sleepwear if you're planning a winter visit.

Even in summer (December–February), temperatures in the south stay chilly. In the middle of the country, summer days can be sunny and warm, or overcast and windy.

Further north, in Auckland and Northland, summers are beautiful. Though the weather can be great during the first half of January, cafes and restaurants tend to be closed while Kiwis go on holiday.

Try to visit during one of the shoulder seasons, Spring (September–November) or Autumn (March–May), when there should be less tourists, lower prices for accommodation, and less extreme temperatures. However, don't let the weather forecast fool you: weather can and will change dramatically.

Where to Stay

Whether you drive a rental on the right side of the road or hike hut-to-hut in the backcountry, there are a variety of ways to explore the wilderness of New Zealand.

Mt Arthur Hut, Kahurangi National Park

i-Sites

Nearly every town in New Zealand has an information center, called the i-Site. Start here if you're looking for accommodation options and to pick up brochures, maps, or get advice from staff. Plus, booking tours through the i-Site will get you discounts.

Eco-friendly methods

Tourism New Zealand uses an environmental labelling badge called Qualmark to help you identify sustainable businesses. Keep your eye out for the green "Enviro Award" fern when booking accommodation and tours.

DOCs campsites

New Zealand's Department of Conservation (DOC) manages over 200 campsites. Book your sites in advance if you're traveling during peak season (October–April).

You can save up to 50% on fees if you buy a weekly campervan pass. Some remote sites operate on a trust-system collection box, but don't skip out on the fees – your money keeps DOC funded!

For a complete list of options, download the CamperMate app. It shows you all the camping sites in a selected map area, organized by Free, low-cost, or paid campgrounds.

Hotels and hostels

If you're interested in finding a conveniently-located hotel instead of a remote hut, booking.com is popular in New Zealand. For a tighter budget, check hostelworld.com. If you're looking for a deal, consider buying a backpacker's network membership through one of these websites: The Youth Hostel Association (YHA), BBH World Travelers Accommodation, BASE Jumping Pass, or Nomads Bed Hopper Pass.

AirBnb and couchsurfing

Kiwis are some of the most hospitable, generous people in the world. Couchsurfing.com or WWOOFing.nz are great ways to hang out with locals.

AirBnB also offers options for authentic Kiwi living. Stay on an estate in the vineyards of Marlborough, or in a glass-walled home in the suburbs of Queenstown. Look for the ones with outdoor hot tubs – New Zealand is great for stargazing!

Hut to hut hiking

DOC maintains a network of over 950 backcountry huts throughout New Zealand's 13 National Parks, and all eight of the Great Walks. The huts vary in amenities, but most have a big bunk bed and a wood-burning stove.

Don't skip the park visitor center. You need to book your nights in advance between October–April. Plus, DOC officials are there to help you prep for your adventure.

Weather forecasts, trail conditions, and other information could be critical to your safety. If you're taking more difficult, remote routes, consider renting a safety beacon before leaving.

Getting Around

If you're short on time, catching a flight from Auckland to Christchurch is the best way to see both islands. However, flights aren't cheap, and you'll miss the best part: landscapes! Opting for a hire car or traveling by campervan might be costly, but it's totally worth it.

Train in Taieri gorge

Which hire car is right for you?

New Zealand is easily explored with a rental car. Many points of interest are difficult to get to without your own vehicle.

JUCY is New Zealand's iconic rental company. Their purple and green rentals can be picked up and dropped off at any airport in New Zealand. They offer a diverse fleet of vehicles, notably the backpacker's basic "el cheapo" option. You can also get deals from partner tour companies in New Zealand just by flashing your JUCY keychain!

There are other rental options too, so shop around online.

Maui and Britz are the most popular options for larger-sized campers. Take care when navigating New Zealand's narrow roads in these big buddies. They're more expensive than smaller options, but opting for a self-contained vehicle may end up saving you money on accommodation.

Travel by coach

Getting around New Zealand on a bus is a safe and enjoyable way to take in the dramatic landscapes without the responsibilities of self-driving. It's cheap, which means it's also a great way to meet other backpackers!

The Kiwi Experience and Stray coaches are popular buses to travel with. Their smaller buses allow them to take the smaller, scenic routes. There are many options, so shop around for

> " New Zealand is easily explored with a rental car. Many points of interest are difficult to get to without your own vehicle.

a company that suits your itinerary and budget.

Travel by train

New Zealand has three options for rail travel.

The Northern Explorer goes straight through the North Island, from Auckland to Wellington.

The Coastal Pacific runs down the east coast of the South Island, from Picton to Christchurch (currently out-of-service, but expected to return mid-2018).

Or, the TranzAlpine – which is one of the most scenic train routes in the world – connecting Christchurch and Greymouth by traversing the South Island's Southern Alps mountain range.

Travel by boat

The Interislander Ferry offers five daily departure times to get between Wellington on the North Island, and Picton on the South. Bundle up and spend a few minutes on the top deck while cruising through the Picton's Marlborough Sounds – there's a good chance you'll see some wildlife!

New Zealand's prized Fiordland National Park holds even more opportunities to marvel at native wildlife. You can choose from Milford, Doubtful, or Dusky Sound. Depending on what type of adventure you're after, booking a full-day or overnight cruise is the best way to fully experience the magic of the fiords.

Buying a Car or Campervan

If you're traveling for more than a month or two, it might be cheaper to buy rather than rent a car or campervan. Given the number of backpackers coming in and out of NZ, there are very often older and well-priced vehicles available. If you think this option is for you, start your search at hostel noticeboards in major cities like Auckland, Christchurch, or Wellington, before moving on to online auction sites. Make sure your vehicle has a current Warrant of Fitness (WoF), a valid registration for the duration of your trip, and don't drive unless you have a valid licence!

Freedom Camping and DOCs Campsites

Even though New Zealand is super relaxed, it rightly enforces camping restrictions. Contrary to popular belief, you can't just camp or park anywhere.

The joy of visiting New Zealand is found in its untouched beauty and innocence – attributes that wouldn't last long without structure and rules. New Zealand's Department of Conservation has numerous campsites on both islands, many of which cost US $9 (NZ $13) per person per night.

Because they're government operated, they are always excellently located, have up to date and well looked after clean facilities, and plenty of space. Do your bit to leave it the same way it was when you arrived – better yet, pick up rubbish if you see it lying around.

Food and Nightlife

By now you're aware New Zealand is a haven for adventure, but what happens once the sun goes down? From quirky, hole-in-the-wall burger joints in Queenstown to shipping container bars in Christchurch, there's something for everyone.

Food foraging

New Zealand has the perfect climate to grow produce year-round. Make the most of it by picking your own sun-ripened fruit and vegetables – which you can do cheaply, or even for free!

Auckland's Kelmarna Gardens in Grey Lynn has some of the most sought after vintage fruit trees and organic crops. Christchurch has The (Edible) Garden City, which hosts events such as "Secretive Porcini Hunting" and a regular "Foragers Feast". Wellington has abundant blackberry bushes in Wadestown, and Dunedin is known for

Queen Street, Auckland

its plentiful amount of edible seaweed.

When foraging in New Zealand, follow the rule of thirds: A portion for yourself, a portion for others, and a portion to ensure crop regeneration. If you want to eat your weight in strawberries though, check out Phil Greig Strawberry Gardens in Kumeu, Auckland.

> From shipping crate cafes to The Pedal Pusher "cycling bar", Christchurch utilized Kiwi ingenuity to pump life back into the city.

Unique nightlife

After the devastating Christchurch earthquakes, the city forged a brand new nightlife strip along the Avon River. From shipping crate cafes to The Pedal Pusher "cycling bar", Christchurch utilized Kiwi ingenuity to pump life back into the city.

There's even a new converted bus bar, Smash Palace – it's concept is similar to the Norwegian "Russ Bus" tradition, where old buses are transformed into hip party venues.

Paua shells

tasted – not to mention the colossal squid cone!

Queenstown must-eats

Heading south, check into Queenstown's famous Fergburger for a beer-battered fish burger, onion rings, and twice-cooked chips. It's cheap, delicious, and portions are beyond generous. It's the perfect meal after a busy day exploring. To skip the queue, phone Ferg's beforehand to place your order.

Traditional Maori "Kai"

Modern NZ cuisine is a mix of international ingredients and flavors, showcased by many innovative, world-class restaurants throughout the country. But traditional Maori ingredients like kumara (sweet potato), whitebait, manuka, and Pikopiko (fern shoots) are still used and loved today.

For the adventurous foodie, the NZ Wild Foods Festival in Hokitika (held every March) is a must. You'll get to try all kinds of Maori dishes like possum meat, huhu grubs, or Kānga kōpiro: a fermented corn dish known colloquially as "Maori porridge".

For something a little more celebratory, don't miss the "Hangi". This traditional cooking method involves wrapping different meats (like chicken and lamb) and root vegetables in leaves and placed in in a pit filled with hot rocks. In areas of high geothermal activity, it can also be cooked using hot steam. The Hangi is best experienced as part of a Maori Cultural Evening in Mitai or Tamaki, Rotorua

The best time to visit Queenstown for vibrant nightlife is late June. The city's surrounded by snow-dusted mountains, spirits are high, and you can cozy up by a roaring fire and drink happy hour hot toddies, after skiing.

If you're planning to visit during the 22nd to the 25th, then you'll also want to catch the Queenstown Winter Festival.

Auckland eateries

Auckland will leave you spoilt for choice with a vast array of top notch eateries. Ponsonby Road serves delicious Asian-fusion cuisine at Moo Chow Chow, Kingsland offers vegan smoothies and Buddha bowls at Mondays, and City Works Depot and &Sushi sell cheap, pick-your-own gourmet sushi.

If you're after a sweet treat in downtown Auckland, Giapo is not your typical ice creamery. Imagine a discombobulating menu of jacket potatoes, gyoza dumplings, and arancini made out of the smoothest, richest ice-cream flavors you've ever

Travel Safety

New Zealand is prone to natural disasters, winding roads, and dangerous activities. On the plus side, the locals are awfully friendly, so crime and scams aren't so much a worry. Here's what you need to know before you go.

Marta Kulesza

Seeking extreme adventure

So, you want to go bungee jumping, sandboarding, and jet boating in New Zealand? The more extreme the sport, the greater the risk of accident or death. But, you know that, right?

Do your research on various different adventure tour operators before you pay the price – literally. Generally speaking, adventure activities in New Zealand will not come cheap, but they'll come with a whole rush of adrenaline.

Weigh up the pros and cons. Are you trying to prove something to a mate? Are you really excited by taking part in the activity? If you answered yes to the first and no to the second, back away. Save your money for something else.

Always read your travel insurance policy wording carefully to know what is and isn't covered.

Safety on the mountains

The Mountain Safety Council of New Zealand offers five tips for safety when doing anything in the rocky peaks above:

- Tell someone where you're going.
- Pack for changing, cold weather.
- Bring supplies.
- Give yourself enough time.
- Don't push yourself.

The council recommends taking a communication device designed for backcountry transmission, like a mountain radio or transceiver. Also consider a Personal Locator Beacon, which sends off an UHF radio signal to let rescuers know where you are.

Earthquakes

New Zealand's greatest natural disaster risk comes in the form of earthquakes, due to its location in an area of seismic shift. While there's no way to predict when a large earthquake will strike, if you're there when one does occur, follow these rules:

> "
> Do your research on various different adventure tour operators before you pay the price – literally.

14

• If you're outside or very close to an exit, move to an open space away from hazards like buildings, trees, powerlines, and bridges, and get on the ground. Make sure your head is covered.

• If you're not close to an exit, it's better to find a safe place inside and ride it out. Look for a place away from falling objects and crouch to the ground, covering your head.

• After the earthquake, go to your evacuation point and try to get in touch with your embassy and emergency contact. Save your phone's battery and let your emergency contact keep friends and family posted.

• If you're trapped under rubble, avoid moving to save your energy, and avoid stirring up dust. Only call for help when you can hear people nearby.

If you're unsure, follow the example of locals.

Road safety

With New Zealand's rugged terrain, it's no surprise the country has some dangerous roads. Never drive tired, never go over the speed limit, and always remember to drive on the right-hand side of the road.

There are many one-way bridges in New Zealand, and it can be easy for left-hand drivers to automatically exit the bridge on the wrong side. Always pay attention to signage.

When you drive on rural roads, you have another living creature to look out for altogether: sheep. They'll stroll nonchalantly out into the road, and

> With New Zealand's rugged terrain, it's no surprise the country has some dangerous roads.

they'll move on by their own accord. Use this time to pull over for a picture.

Never pull over to take pictures where it's unsafe. This is a major cause of accidents, especially in places like Milford Sound or the road to Mount Cook. Great photo opportunities, not many safe places to pull over. There'll be time for photos when you get there.

Visas for New Zealand

Australian residents or citizens will not require a visa to visit New Zealand, but you will need to make sure your passport is valid for at least three months longer than the expected departure date.

For US citizens with a valid passport, your first three months in New Zealand will not require a visa. You can apply for more time at the border, but no more than six months for any 12-month period.

UK citizens (or passport holders) can stay up to six months without a visa.

If you're not an Australian, UK, or US citizen, you may need a visa. Apply here: https://www.immigration.govt.nz/new-zealand-visas

Entry to New Zealand

New Zealand is place of delicate ecosystems. Offenders will be handed a stiff fine, and anyone who fails to declare fresh produce, seeds, or pets upon arrival will be handed prison time. Items can, and often are, seized.

It's best to check in with the Biosecurity New Zealand website: http://www.mpi.govt.nz/

If you're bringing worn-in hiking boots, keep them at the top of your bag and take them out to be inspected. The environment here thrives because of their strict rules, so don't be 'that guy'.

NORTH ISLAND

From Cape Reinga in the north to Cape Palliser down south, make the North Island your destination for wine, culture, geo-thermal pools, sand dunes, volcanic peaks, and forests.

Auckland

Many visitors rush out of the city for postcard views further south. But, if you know where to look in Auckland, you'll find some of the most mind-blowingly photogenic sites, tasty local food, and an introduction to Kiwi culture.

Typical tourist sites

If you're staying in the center of the city, Auckland's tourist tick-list is within walking distance. Nip up the Sky Tower for a bird's eye view, and wander down to Wynyard Quarter to understand why Auckland used to be called the 'City of Sails'.

The Auckland Museum gives a great introduction to Maori culture, and the park it's located in (the Auckland Domain) is picnic perfection. Don't miss the Auckland Art Gallery on the way there.

If Auckland is your only destination, get a taste for bungee jumping off the Auckland Harbor Bridge – otherwise, save your pennies for the more storied and scenic bungees in Taupo or Queenstown.

Local's top picks for inner-city Auckland

For views, take a 15-minute ferry from the downtown terminal to Devonport. From there, walk up North Head – an extinct grassy volcano on the North Shore's tip. The islands of the Hauraki Gulf dominate the seascape, and the city's iconic skyline looms large in the other direction. Explore the old war tunnels built into the hillside, and pop down the hill to Devonport or Cheltenham for a swim.

If you're around from December–March, check out the event guide for Silo Park. Built for the 2011 Rugby World Cup, Silo Park is Auckland's summer hotspot for outdoor gigs, movies, and markets.

> The Auckland Museum gives a great introduction to Maori culture, and the park it's located in (the Auckland Domain) is picnic perfection.

Sky Tower bungee

Waitakere Ranges and Piha

West of city lies the Waitakere Ranges (the Waitaks, in local speak). Start your adventure with the 45-minute drive to Piha (pronounced Pee-ha), arguably New Zealand's most beautiful beach.

Don't let any weather put you off. If it's sunny, great. If not, even better. Piha is a driftwood-strewn, black-sand beach with thundering surf – it's best in wet, windy weather.

First, enjoy the view from the lookout on the road that winds down into town. If you're keen to stretch your legs, take the Kitekite track to Kitekite Falls. The vegetation in this area is beautiful, studded with nikau palms, fern fronds, and native birds, and the falls at the end of the track are worth the walk. The Piha Café is a great place to refuel after a swim or a blustery beach or bush walk.

While you're in the area, escape the crowds at one of the stunning, but seldom-visited, beaches nearby – Anawhata is the best of the bunch. It's a steep (but well-maintained) walk from the carpark down to the beach, and you'll likely be the only people there.

For a full day walk, drive to Huia, and take on the Omanawanui Track – Auckland's best day walk. The track traverses the narrow ridge separating bushy hills from the Manukau Harbor. You'll undulate gradually down to Whatipu, a wild beach that forms the tip of the Waitaks. Combine that with the Kura Track to get back to your car, and you've got a day trip that takes in the best of the west coast.

Pack supplies: There are no shops

Waitakere Ranges Regional Park

or cafes at Whatipu, but you can reward yourself with a stop at the Huia Foodstore afterwards (home to the country's best chocolate caramel slice).

Waiheke Island

For sunbathing, art, and wine, head straight to Waiheke. It's 35 minutes from the downtown ferry terminal, and has a network of public buses once you're on the island. Cool off in the sea at Oneroa Beach, Palm Beach or Onetangi.

The best viewpoints in the island are occupied by vineyards – if you're staying central, taste the local drop at Cable Bay or Mudbrick, but if you've got a car to explore with, take in the sights at the lesser-known Te Whau or Man O' War.

If you're visiting over summer, don't miss Sculpture on the Gulf – an outdoor sculpture trail on the cliffs about Matiatia Bay.

Rangitoto and Motutapu

Almost every view in inner-city Auckland looks across to Rangitoto, a round volcano that looks the same no matter which direction you view it from. It's a great day trip from the

If you're visiting over summer, don't miss Sculpture on the Gulf – an outdoor sculpture trail on the cliffs about Matiatia Bay.

Coromandel

downtown ferry terminal – sail across in the morning, hike to the top from great views over the gulf, and sail back in the afternoon. Take a head torch and stop in at the lava caves on the way down.

Motutapu Island isn't serviced by ferries regularly, but it's connected by bridge to Rangitoto, and it only takes a few hours to hike across. Take a tent and camp at Home Bay, and explore the island's many trails.

Tiritiri Matangi

Bird lovers, head to Tiritiri Matangi, an open wildlife sanctuary in the north of the Hauraki Gulf. New Zealand's native bird population was devastated by the introduction of pests, but it's now blossoming again on Tiritiri Matangi – thanks to a huge conservation effort. You might even spot a Takahe – a flightless bird once thought to be extinct, but now number just over 300.

Hobbiton

Venture south of Auckland and you'll soon find yourself in tranquil Waikato farmland, home to Hobbiton. To visit Hobbiton, you'll need to book a guided tour from Matamata, Rotorua, or The Shire's Rest – a gorgeous converted woolshed that serves as the entrance to the movie set. If you're planning on visiting Mount Maunganui or Rotorua, you could fit a visit in on your way.

Raglan

Surfers and beach-lovers, take a road trip to Raglan on the west coast, two hours south of Auckland. It's home to some of New Zealand's best surf breaks, and the cute town center is full of funky art galleries and cafés.

Coromandel

Within a two-hour drive from Auckland, you'll also find the Coromandel Peninsula. It's full of beautiful hiking trails and white-sand beaches. For swimming, don't miss Hahei and Cathedral Cove, Hot Water Beach, or New Chums. For a day walk with great views of the peninsula, head up The Pinnacles.

> " Surfers and beach-lovers, take a road trip to Raglan on the west coast, two hours south of Auckland. It's home to some of New Zealand's best surf breaks.

Sport, Music, and Culture

Eden Park is New Zealand's sporting ground zero, home to the famous All Blacks. If you're lucky enough to be there when a game is on and there are tickets left, snap them up.

Cricket is the country's summer game. If you're new to the sport, try a T20 game (they only last about four hours) or a one-dayer (you'll be done in eight hours). Enjoy the relaxed spirit of the summer game; lounge around in the sunshine, enjoy good food, and great company.

For local music, head to K Road (technically Karangahape Road, but that's a mouthful, even for the locals). Neck of the Woods and The Wine Cellar showcase local talent as well as big name international acts. For something more chilled, the Tuning Fork, next to the huge Vector Arena, is a prime spot for jazz, country, and folk performers.

Get a feel for Maori culture in the Auckland Museum, and keep an eye out for information dotted all around the city's surrounds. Maori legends add a layer of beauty to the area's wild landscapes and playful birdlife.

19

Wellington

One of the great things about Wellington is that it doesn't really have typical tourist spots. Most travelers to New Zealand aren't here for the cities, which has left Wellington in the hands of the locals.

Wellington

Must see and do around town

Check out New Zealand's national museum, Te Papa, which is a local treasure. *Lord of the Rings* fans should head out to Weta Studios to see how the movies were made, and even hop on a tour to some of the local filming locations.

Either drive or walk up Mt. Victoria, a lovely green park in the center of town that has heaps of trails and tracks and fabulous views of the city.

Wellington for foodies

If you want to experience Wellington like a local, give yourself time to check out some of the great foodie spots all around town. Wander through the CBD and keep an eye out for hidden street art, and if you find yourself in the city on a Sunday, pop down to the harborside market next to Te Papa which sells local produce, but also has an array of delightful street carts and food trucks.

There's a delicious night market every Friday night on Cuba Street, Wellington's iconic hipster street full of local shops, speakeasy bars, restaurants, and delicious cafes.

Wellington's coffee scene is world-

renowned, so be sure to grab a local flat white when you're in town.

Zealandia

Catch a ride on the classic red cable car from the Wellington CBD to the Botanical Gardens before hopping on a shuttle out to Zealandia, a predator-free, fenced eco-sanctuary.

Once you walk through the gates, it truly feels like you have not only left Wellington behind but also have stepped into another world. Before humans arrived in New Zealand, there were no mammals, only birds and a couple of bats, and Zealandia is working towards protecting many of the native New Zealand species, including the iconic Kiwi bird which you can often see on a night tour.

Mount Kaukau

One of the highest points near

> 66
>
> There's a delicious night market every Friday night on Cuba Street, Wellington's iconic hipster street full of local shops, speakeasy bars, restaurants, and delicious cafes.

Wellington is the secret spot of Mount Kaukau near Khandallah, just outside of town. A climb to the top will reward you with some of the best views of Wellington, and it's the perfect place for a picnic.

Red Rocks reserve

Just like it sounds, the Red Rocks is a coastal zone with walks and notably red rocks – a great weekend escape from downtown Wellington.

With such rugged coastlines nearby, it's worth wandering around the local coastal walks and even visit the local fur seal colony – though don't get too close. Check out the local cafes and walks along the nearby Lyall and Island Bays.

Somes Island

Somes Island, in the Wellington harbor, is a scenic reserve that's home to penguins and weta, among many other native New Zealand creatures. Once a quarantine island, now there are short walks and you can even camp here overnight after catching a ferry over.

Martinborough and the Wairarapa

The boutique wine growing region of the Wairarapa is just north of Wellington and home to some charming little towns and vineyards with a growing gourmet scene. Many of the wineries are close to each other, and it's great fun to rent a bike and cycle between them.

In spring, it's home to a festival called Toast Martinborough that takes place

Hiking up to Mt Victoria

across many of the vineyards, with live music and great food. Tickets sell out super-fast to Wellington locals who return year after year.

Kapiti Island

An hour's drive north of Wellington will bring you to the stunning Kapiti Coast, where you can catch a quick boat ride over to Kapiti Island, another nature reserve home to some of New Zealand's great endangered species.

The number of people allowed on the island is limited per day. But, for the best experience, you should stay overnight. You can even go glamping there, so check out your options and book ahead – this is a year-round destination that books out fast.

There are plenty of walking trails on the island, but the best would have to be summiting Tuteremoana. At 1,709ft (521m), this is the highest point on the island, so you're guaranteed spectacular views.

Kiwis (the bird, not the people) are nocturnal, and you'll often hear them at night on Kapiti, and even see one if you're lucky.

> "
> The boutique wine growing region of the Wairarapa is just north of Wellington and home to some charming little towns and vineyards with a growing gourmet scene.

Rotorua and Taupo

Dip your toes into the hot sands of Lake Taupo, experience geothermal wonders at Rotorua, and explore the Redwoods at Whakarewarewa Forest.

Champagne Pool at Waiotapu Thermal Wonderland, Rotorua

Thermal wonders

Find a local kayak group and set ship to the waters of Orakei Korako, or Hidden Valley, between Taupo and Rotorua. The steaming, colorful silica terraces and geysers are a spectacular sight, and the area is riddled with fascinating volcanic and geothermal features, from huge active volcanoes to hot springs and boiling mud.

Check out Wai-O-Tapu to see the most vibrant, colorful pools and craters, including the often-photographed, 900-year-old Champagne Pool. Visit Hell's Gate Geothermal Park and Mud Spa, where you can indulge in a family mud bath. Be sure to check out Te Whakarewarewa, the living Maori village where geothermal field Te Puia boasts the largest active geyser in the southern hemisphere, Pōhutu.

If it's thermal luxury you're after, head to the famed Poynesian Spa in central Rotorua.

Hot pools without tourists

You only need to drive into Rotorua and see the steam emitting from the drains – and breathe in the sulphur – to realize you've entered a live geothermal field with a city on top.

Steam and spouting hot water are a normal everyday presence, and Rotorua once supplied the hot water to be used domestically. However, by the late 1980s, all bores were required to close as the aquifers were being depleted. Occasionally, an old bore still erupts in central Rotorua – or a new geyser appears naturally on the outskirts. Such is life on an active volcano.

The hot foot bath is at Kuirau Park. At first glance, this ordinary-looking public park is just that, but a quick investigation of the fenced areas demonstrates the activity happening just below your feet, with boiling mud and steaming vents.

If immersing just your feet isn't enough, drive south to Wai-O-Taupo and follow the locals (or do a quick internet search) to the hot waterfall just past Lady Knox Geyser.

> " Steam and spouting hot water are a normal everyday presence, and Rotorua once supplied the hot water to be used domestically.

Alternatively, turn off just before Wai-O-Tapu and follow the Kerosene Creek sign to two warm waterfalls. These are naturally heated, so exercise common sense and test the water temperature first.

Taupo

While Rotorua is considered New Zealand's geothermal capital, smaller Taupo is worth a visit. Situated on Lake Taupo – the crater of a super volcano – the whole town looks toward the snow-capped peaks of three active volcanoes: Tongariro, Ruapehu, and Ngauruhoe.

Just north of Taupo is another geothermal field called Craters of the Moon, where there's also jet boating, trout fishing, and bungee jumping.

Take a dip in the hot waterfall of Otumuheke Stream at Spa Park, where locals submerge themselves with a cold beer in hand, and contemplate the swirling Waikato River. The stream mixes with cool river water, so there's a temperature to suit everyone.

As you dig your toes into the layers of volcanic pumice on Lake Taupo's shoreline, feel the hot water heat up the soles of your feet. A number of warm streams also flow into the main lake, bridged by the sealed, scenic track along the lakefront. All this makes for pleasant swimming temperatures year-round.

Thermal wonders in winter

Rotorua in winter is arguably more spectacular than in summer, not only because there are less crowds, but increased rainfall naturally enhances geothermal activity. On a cold, frosty morning, steam enveloping the town creates a unique, spooky atmosphere.

If you're done soaking yourself in hot pools during the coldest months of the year (what could be better?) and a breath of fresh air from the sulphur is in order, the Redwoods, or Whakarewarewa Forest, is a complete contrast.

Escape into towering stands of Californian Coastal Redwoods, just minutes from the CBD to walk, mountain bike, or run its 56mi (90km) of trails and enjoy the views.

Alternatively, head south for the ski fields of Whakapapa and Turoa on Mt Ruapehu. On your way, you'll pass through Turangi (there's more hot pools here at Tokaanu, and world class trout fishing) before passing Mt Tongariro's steaming vents and a saddle draped in ancient forests.

Whakapapa is more accessible and has a sealed road leading to the base, making it the busier of the two. Turoa, near Ohakune, is generally quieter, and has New Zealand's highest chairlift.

> On a cold, frosty morning, steam enveloping the town creates a unique, spooky atmosphere.

Pohutu Geyser

Northland

Head to the Far North and Bay of Islands to hear stories about legends of the land, see where the nation was born, and explore isolated bays north of Auckland.

You could just stop in to see the highlights of Northland: 90 Mile Beach, Waitangi Treaty Grounds, Waipoua Kauri Tree forest, and Hole in the Rock. But, if you're ready for the adventure, indulge in these lesser-known experiences.

Matai Bay, Northland

Martina Grassi

Visiting Northland

Cape Reinga (*Te Rerenga Wairua* in Te Reo Māori), is not only the most north-western point of New Zealand, it's also one of the most sacred spots in the country. With plenty of beaches and rugged coastlines to explore, this region is an awesome destination to soak up the sun and learn where 'The Nation' was born.

Watch the sunset at Cape Reinga

Standing at the most sacred place in Aotearoa, watch the sun set over the hills and listen to the sound of the wind and the ocean slamming into the coast. This is where the ancient pohutukawa tree stands, and the spirits take the leap to go back to their ancestral home.

It's a six hour drive from Auckland on route nr1 – this is the only road that crosses Northland's region in full. Once you're there, take a ten-minute walk

from the carpark to the lighthouse.

This is a sacred place in Māori tradition, and you're not allowed to eat or drink here. It goes without saying, you should always show respect to local beliefs and customs.

It can get pretty crowded around lunch, when the tourist buses get there, so plan to arrive in time for sunrise or sunset to avoid the crowds.

Give yourself a few days to drive nr10 and stop in to explore remote bays, like Spirits Bay and Matai Bay. If you find a campsite along the way, be responsible and practice "leave no trace" camping rules.

Camping in Matai Bay

On the Karikari peninsula, Matai Bay is worth the detour. Whether you go camping by the beach or choose to walk or climb to see unparalleled panoramic views of the landscapes all

> " This is a sacred place in Māori tradition, and you're not allowed to eat or drink here. It goes without saying, you should always show respect to local beliefs and customs.

24

around, there's no way you'd regret checking this place out.

Spend a day in Otehei Bay

After finding solitude in the remote bays of the Far North, head to Paihia. This spot might be the main tourist hub in the Bay of Islands, but a visit will prove why it gets the hype.

Bring on subtropical weather and sunny pristine beaches as you choose from one of 100+ islands to go island hopping (for approximately US $70/NZ $100).

Hop into a public water taxi (US $17 for a return fare) to get to Urupukapuka Island and explore Otehei Bay for the day. From the island, you'll catch a sunset with a panoramic view of the beach and other islands around.

If you choose to camp on Urupukapuka Island, bring your own camping gear, hiking shoes to explore the island's tracks, food, sunscreen, insect repellent, and small change. The campsites are very basic and have no power. It's recommended to book ahead (you can do so through the DOCs website).

Donket Bay

Donkey Bay

Don't miss dropping into Russell – the historic town where the first European settlement took place. Take a 20 minute walk from the main street to Long Beach, where you'll find local families relaxing on the sand or trying their best at water sports.

Nearby, you'll find Donkey Bay – an "unofficial" nudist beach. If you choose to visit, show respect to those around you. If it's not your cup of tea, head back to Long Beach.

Panoramic views from Mount Parihaka

If you're heading to Whangarei, don't miss Mount Parihaka scenic reserve.

Take the summit track to see panoramic views of town, but stay a while – there's so much more to this place. The Māori made their most important fortress here, and, at the summit, there's a World War II Memorial.

This is an easy track, but you should allow two hours for the return hike.

> 66
> Bring on subtropical weather and sunny pristine beaches as you choose from one of 100+ islands to go island hopping.

Otehei Bay

25

SOUTH ISLAND

Small coastal towns, rigorous multi-day hikes, New Zealand's highest peak, and some of the most incredible scenery can be found on the South Island. But, you already know that, right? From Abel Tasman to Stewart Island, here's how to make the most of your adventure.

Queenstown

Often referred to as the Adventure Capital of the World, Queenstown offers something for every age, every adrenaline requirement, and – quite importantly – for every budget.

Free adventures around Queenstown

Hiking is an activity that everyone can afford, and it goes hand in hand with photography. Combine the two and you get an awesome experience on a very low budget!

The most popular hike in Queenstown is the route up Ben Lomond. For experienced hikers, plan your summit in time for sunrise. Waking up in the early hours to start hiking isn't easy, but sitting on the top of the mountain watching the sun rising makes it all worth it.

If you're after a less strenuous, free activity, then a round of frisbee golf at Queenstown Gardens, followed by an ice cream on the beach while watching the sunset is hard to beat.

Queenstown and the Remarkables

Pricey experiences that are totally worth it

Did you know Queenstown is the birthplace of commercial bungee jumping? It all started at the famous Kawarau Bridge with one crazy guy, and now a company, called AJ Hackett. Now they have three bungies around town, all with different heights, scariness levels (technical term), and prices. If that's not enough, there's also the world's longest Canyon Swing!

The Queenstown Ledge is perched 984ft (300m) above Queenstown's skyline, and is the jump with the highest dropout rate. Up for a challenge? Do it at dusk when the town's lights start to flicker below!

Skydiving is another adrenaline-filled activity popular in Queenstown. Jumping out at 15,000ft (4,572m) over the snow-capped Remarkables Mountain Range is an experience that

" Jumping out at 15,000ft (4,572m) over the snow-capped Remarkables Mountain Range is an experience that can satisfy even the diehard adrenaline junkies.

27

Queenstown and Lake Wakitipu

Sam Grimmer

can satisfy even the diehard adrenaline junkies.

Still looking for an adrenaline rush? Don't just feel the spray from the Shotover Jet, go river boarding in the Kawarau River. You'll get a rush swimming through rapids, surfing the waves, and riding whirlpools.

Day trips to smaller towns

There are two nearby towns that are totally worth a visit. The first, Arrowtown, is a quaint little village which boasts some renowned restaurants and bars. Arrowtown is also home to rich history, as it's where the gold rush of the 19th century was focused.

Glenorchy is a one-hour drive north of Queenstown along the Glenorchy-Queenstown Road – one of the most scenic roads in the entire country. The town is host to famous photography spots, such as the Glenorchy Pier and a few exquisite hikes.

The Routeburn, one of New Zealand's Great Walks starts here, and so does the route up Mount Alfred.

Winter in Queenstown

The Remarkables form the backdrop to many pictures of Queenstown, and views from your plane window will surely get you excited as you fly over Lake Wakatipu.

If you've got the extra time and a hire-car (or pay for the shuttle service) take the trip to Cardrona, approximately one and a half hours (give or take traffic and time putting the chains on your wheels). Here, you'll find more advanced runs compared to the Remarkables.

From the center of town, it should only take forty minutes to drive up to The Remarkables Ski Area where there are a number of trails for both advanced and beginners.

Be sure to check out prices from a variety of snow gear rental companies in town, and make sure they don't rush you out the door without checking to see your equipment fits well.

> 66
> The Remarkables form the backdrop to many pictures of Queenstown, and views from your plane window will surely get you excited as you fly over Lake Wakatipu.

Christchurch

Community efforts and lots of construction work helped Christchurch emerge from the rubble and turn into a vibrant and creative city. Whether you prefer adventure, dining, shopping, or art, Christchurch has something for everyone.

Gap Fillers project

The Gap Fillers project started as an urban regeneration initiative to showcase a range of projects, events, and things to see and do around Christchurch, and literally fills up the gaps left behind after the earthquakes.

Check out the outdoor Dance-O-Mat, book-exchange corners, and a giant-size Super Street Arcade on the corner of Tuam Street in Christchurch Central.

Street art

Street art is also a big part of Christchurch, and a way to bring the city back to life. Local and international artists have created vibrant murals throughout the city. Go on a graffiti-hunt

Cardboard Cathedral, Christchurch

Regent Street, Christchurch

and be amazed by what you find.

Check out Cathedral Square, the corner of Manchester and Welles Street, Colombo Street, Tuam Street, the top end of High Street, and Madras Street. This map shows where to find street art: https://watchthisspace.org.nz/

Cardboard Cathredral

One of Christchurch's main attractions is the Cardboard Cathedral, which was built when the original one got destroyed in the earthquake. It's called that, because the foundations are made out of cardboard, and it's a must-see when you're here.

Museums and exhibitions

Art-lovers can discover the newest exhibitions at the public Art Gallery Te Puna o Waiwhetu (free entry), or learn more about the earthquakes at the Quake City Museum. The CoCa gallery

> 66
> One of Christchurch's main attractions is the Cardboard Cathedral, which was built when the original one got destroyed in the earthquake.

showcases contemporary art to provoke conversation among visitors.

Water sports

If you're into water sports, you can go surfing in Sumner, rafting on the Rangitata Gorge, or jet boating on the Waimakariri River just outside of Christchurch.

Hiking in the Port Hills

If you prefer to stay out of water, there's great climbing in the Port Hills, with easy to difficult routes.

There are also many short and rewarding hikes with beautiful views, like the steep Rapaki Track. Taylors Mistake is a great walk along the coast, and also good for fishing!

For longer walks and overnight huts, the Banks Peninsula is the place to be.

Difficult tracks in Arthur's Pass

If you're looking for more intense hikes, Castle Hill and Arthur's Pass will be worth the two-hour drive from town. Try out local favorites Castle Hill Peak, Avalanche Peak, or the Bealey Spur. Castle Hill is also great for bouldering and climbing.

Thrill-seekers will love Cave Stream, where you follow a river through a cave. You don't need to be experienced, but don't go by yourself!

Tip: Always check the weather and water level, and take a head torch with you, because it's pitch black inside.

Mountainbiking

Christchurch's surround hills are also great for mountain biking. Rent a bike

Castle Hill

Pennaz Bilimoria

and ride one of the many tracks in the Port Hills or in Bottle Lake Forest. For a more leisurely bike ride, cycle the Little River Trail.

Christchurch for foodies

You'll find many unique cafes and restaurants in Christchurch. After the earthquake, a wave of young, creative entrepreneurs started up their own hospitality businesses, making the city more vibrant and delicious.

Check out Pot Sticker Dumpling Bar, Burgers & Beers, Hello Sunday, Park ranger, and, if you like to see your food delivered to your table through pneumatic tubes, head to C1.

New Regent street is the place to be for cocktails, authentic bars, and fine dining.

Nightlife

More of a night person? There's a lot

> If you're looking for more intense hikes, Castle Hill and Arthur's Pass will be worth the two-hour drive from town.

going on in the evenings. Check out trendy bars like The Last Word, or funky outdoor bar SMASH Palace, the Theatre Royal, or one of the many independent, little cinemas, like Alice Cinematique or Academy Gold.

Lyttelton

Close to Christchurch, you'll find the portside town of Lyttelton. Stroll around the artsy main street, have a beer in the funky bars, and check out the waterfront.

If you're there on a Saturday, check out the Farmers Market. With organic food and live music, it's a must-do.

Akaroa

Take a one-hour drive to Akaroa on the Banks Peninsula. Akaroa is a quirky, historic village with a French influence, so don't be surprised by all the French flags and street names.

Take your time to drive there, as it's one of the most beautiful roads in the area. The picturesque town is also home to penguins, alpacas, and dolphins.

Tip: Stop at the Hilltop Tavern for a drink with a panoramic view.

Castle Hill

Exploring Castle Hill makes for a great day out. For LOTR fans out there, this is where the fellowship were filmed running through the valley of rocks in *The Fellowship of the Ring*.

The strange limestone rock formations look like the ruins of a castle (hence the name). Walk around the rocks, or pack a picnic to take to the top of one. The rocks also offer world-class

bouldering and climbing.

A bit further down the road you'll reach Arthur's Pass National Park, with impressive mountains and beautiful walks.

Waipara Valley

Hankering for a wine? It's always wine time in Waipara Valley, which is great for wine tasting. Visit multiple vineyards, enjoy cellar door tastings, and try some of the delicious food. Often, they've got live bands playing!

Lake Tekapo and Mount Cook: Road-Tripping the Center of the South Island

Christchurch is a very common starting point for road-trippers on the South Island, and if you're road-tripping through the center instead of driving the West Coast, make sure Lake Tekapo and Mount Cook are on your itinerary.

Find local freedom campsites near Tekapo to skip paying high prices for accommodation. Plus, Lake Tekapo is an International Dark Sky Reserve, one of the largest in the world – which makes it one of the best places in New Zealand to camp beneath the stars.

One of the highlights of a visit to Aoraki National Park is hiking the well-trodden Hooker Valley Track. This 3.1mi (5km) return, easy trail starts at White Horse Hill Campground (aka parking lot) and ends at the Hooker Valley Lake at the foot of Mount Cook. Pack a few snacks to enjoy while sitting on the edge of the glacial lake or on one of the tables (if there's room).

Lake Tekapo and Mount Cook

Sam Grimmer

Wanaka

Just a stone's throw away from Queenstown, the resort town of Wanaka is the gateway to Mount Aspiring National Park. This isn't just a prime destination in winter, but a year-round adventurer's paradise.

Cycling around Lake Wanaka

Climbing and biking

In the summer, there's plenty of rock-climbing routes in all grades scattered off the Aspiring Road. Mountain biking trails, including Dean's Bank, and the nearby Cardrona Bike park offers world class, lift-accessed downhill trails.

Paddle and swim

Of course, you've also got Wanaka lake itself to explore. Make the choice between kayaking and SUPing, and go for a guided or self-guided paddle with Paddle Wanaka.

Some local favorite spots to go for a dip are Eely Point and Devil's Elbow. Devil's Elbow is one of the most

Kate McDonald
Blue Pools

powerful rivers in New Zealand, so it's a good idea to wear a lifejacket.

Blue Pools

Looking for an Instagram-worthy swimming hole? Just a short drive from Wanaka is Blue Pools, near Makarora. But be warned, it's cold!

To get to the Blue Pools, you'll walk through moss-covered trees along a gravel pathway and over a wooden walkway, before you reach the first of two suspension bridges.

If it's been raining, chances are these Blue Pools will be closer to murky green – but it's still an awesome spot.

Hiking around Wanaka

Take on the classics such as Roys Peak, Mount Iron, or the other lakeside tracks – including the very short walk from the car park to 'That Wanaka Tree.'

For less crowded trails, head to

> " Looking for an Instagram-worthy swimming hole? Just a short drive from Wanaka is Blue Pools, near Makarora. But be warned, it's cold!

Roy's Peak Wanaka

nearby Mount Aspiring National Park. The trailhead at Raspberry flats (a scenic 31mi/50km drive from the city center), offers some of the region's best tramping. The Rob Roy track is a 6mi (10km) return trail that winds up a steep valley for unparalleled views of a hanging Rob Roy glacier.

Kea are often seen cavorting in the alpine cirque, and sometimes pieces of the glacier will calve away and thunder down onto the rock faces below.

Better yet, for those with the time and gear are tracks that lead further up the main Matukituki Valley to Aspiring Hut and beyond. The well-equipped hut costs US $20 (NZ $30) per night. The smaller and more rustic Cascade Hut (US $7/NZ $10 per night) is an alternative for those wanting to explore the region.

Hardcore trampers can tackle the Liverpool or French Ridge Tracks for a

Winter in Wanaka

With two ski fields – Cardrona and Treble Cone – less than an hour away, Wanaka makes for a top choice when it comes to winter sports.

Treble Cone offers some of the most difficult terrain in New Zealand, as well as the largest vertical drop in the area. Both offer great back-country skiing, and 'flexi-pass' options – where one ticket provides access to both fields.

On the other side of the Cardrona Range road, there's the Snow Farm which offers more than 30mi (50km) of epic cross-country skiing and snow-shoeing, as well as gear rental. It also has two trail-accessed back-country huts for those wanting to experience a real winter wonderland.

Costs are affordable, with a one-day trail pass, rental, and night in a hut coming in at just over US $70 (NZ $100) – about the same cost as a day on the slopes.

The best thing about Wanaka is that on a nice winter's day, most of the summer activities can still be enjoyed – you might just need to wear a puffy.

night at the huts, or add a round trip ascent to Cascade Saddle via the Pylon route, above Aspiring Hut. The route ascends over 4,265ft (1,300m) in a little over 2.5mi (4km) – so it's not for the feint-hearted.

Kaikoura

On the east coast of the New Zealand's South Island, nestled between the wild Pacific Ocean and the Seaward Kaikoura mountains, this small town packs a punch when it comes to adventure and wildlife experiences.

Kaikoura Peninsula

Take the three-hour loop hike along the Kaikoura Peninsula Walkway for a short, informative hike (thanks to information panels along the way). Just be sure to look up every once in a while to spot local wildlife.

Kaikoura Peninsula Walkway

Mount Fyffe

If you're feeling up for the challenge, hike to the summit of Mt Fyffe for the best views of Kaikoura. It'll take eight hours (return) to reach the top, at 5,255ft (1,602m), or five hours to the hut (which also has good views).

Culture in Kaikoura

Kaikoura is home to the people of Ngati

Kuri, a hapu (sub-tribe) of the major South Island iwi (tribe) Ngai Tahu. They own Whale Watch, and their base is the spectacularly-situated Takahanga Marae.

After the earthquake, the marae opened its doors to hundreds of stranded tourists for shelter and food – including Kaikoura's famous crayfish.

Maori Tours Kaikoura offer cultural experiences, including a visit to the marae's beautiful exterior grounds.

Whale watching

For most visitors, Kaikoura is synonymous with whales. Sperm whales are drawn year-round to the undersea Kaikoura Canyon, just 800m offshore. Other whale species are regularly spotted, and you're likely to see dolphins, albatross, and penguins, which are all attracted to the canyon's rich supply of food.

> For most visitors, Kaikoura is synonymous with whales. Sperm whales are drawn year-round to the undersea Kaikoura Canyon, just 800m offshore.

Whale Watch runs several tours per day, on large and comfortable catamarans. Guides seek out whales before bobbing next to them, ready for travelers to snap up their quintessential fluke (tail) photo.

Alternatively – particularly if sea sickness is an issue – take to the air with Wings Over Whales Kaikoura or Kaikoura Helicopters for a birds-eye view.

Wildlife adventures

If you don't mind squeezing into a full-body wetsuit and braving Pacific Ocean temperatures, why not get up close and personal with Kaikoura's resident seals and dolphins?

Seal Swim Kaikoura will take you to snorkel with playful seals among the rocks, while Dolphin Encounter cruises out to meet the permanent population of dusky dolphins and albatross, either from the boat or in the water.

Should your budget not stretch to all this touring, don't worry, there's wildlife everywhere. You'll find the local seal colony and birdlife at the Kaikoura Peninsula – seals are often found

Kaikoura coastline

sunning themselves in the carpark – or just spot them from the highway, preferably on a beach while indulging in some fresh Kaikoura crayfish for lunch.

Kaikoura seals

New Landscapes and Community Efforts After the 2016 Earthquake

The area was hit by a 7.8 magnitude earthquake in November 2016. The earthquake lifted the seafloor by meters off the coast, permanently changing the coastline. Now, visitors have the unique opportunity to see the results of nature's raw power firsthand in the dramatically-changed landscapes.

The Government opened its coffers wide to reinstate Kaikoura's uplifted marina, where tour boats were left stranded. They rebuilt the destroyed State Highway 1 and the railway line between Marlborough and Christchurch – even employing full-time "seal wranglers" to protect the seals that famously live and breed here.

As a silver lining, new and fascinating natural phenomenon were discovered after the quake, including springs bubbling from the seafloor off the Kaikoura Peninsula. Dubbed Hope Springs, they were found by Kaikoura Kayaks' local owner, who now offers guided tours to the site.

Surf breaks around Kaikoura were enhanced by the uplift, particularly at Gooch's Beach, a short stroll from Kaikoura's center.

Also revealed were perfectly spherical rocks, similar to the famous Moeraki Boulders.

Fiordland

While Milford Sound gets the accolades, the entire Fiordland region deserves a little more attention.

Milford Sound
Sam Grimmer

Cruising Milford Sound

Competition and demand have pushed the bottom-end prices of a cruise around the World Heritage site into the realm of affordable, for even the most budget-conscious traveler (prices for a two-hour boat ride start at just US $31), but you might just not get what you expect for your money.

Yes, it is spectacularly beautiful – rain or shine – but with the huge crowds and a parade of vessels, it feels a bit more like the "It's a Small World" ride at Disneyland than a genuine wilderness experience. Here are some alternatives that will be every bit as stunning, but involve far more solitude.

Where to stop off along Milford Road

The 75mi (120km) long Milford Road that leads to Milford Sound has many well-

Falls in Lake Marian

> The 75mi (120km) long Milford Road that leads to Milford Sound has many well-advertised stopping spots such as Mirror lakes, Key Summit, and The Chasm.

advertised stopping spots such as Mirror lakes, Key Summit, and The Chasm.

Like Milford Sound itself, stops here during high season will involve tour busses and shoulder-to-shoulder short walks to pretty scenery where pictures are snapped by the thousands every day. But, the road also contains some less-frequented destinations that are equally spectacular.

Hike up Gertrude Saddle

The hike up to Gertrude Saddle past Black Lake leaves from near the Homer Tunnel, and offers a challenging five to six-hour return trek in unparalleled alpine scenery.

You can camp (for free) at either the saddle or the lake, and even climb Barrier Knob – voted by New Zealanders as the most spectacular mountain that can be climbed without technical equipment.

The Monument, Doubtful Sound

Lake Marian trail

The Lake Marian trail departs from the Hollyford Road, just a stone's throw from the main thoroughfare, but far enough that it receives only a fraction of the visits.

After an hour, this shorter walk leads to a stunning cirque (an amphitheater-like valley formed by glacial erosion) and negotiates hanging boardwalk sections over the frothing Marian Creek.

Falls Creek track

The time crunched can take a quick jaunt up the first kilometer of the Falls Creek Track. The track deteriorates after that, but in a short span will provide some up-close-and-personal (and handrail-free) views of waterfalls tumbling -through the steep landscape.

Another quick option is to follow the Mistake Creek track for fifteen minutes for quick access to an iconic kiwi three-wire bridge.

Doubtful Sound

A trip to Doubtful Sound is another great alternative to Milford – albeit a pricier one, with both cruise and kayaking options available, starting from US $170.

But, because of the remoteness, cruise itineraries in particular leave little time for self-exploration. Travel to Doubtful Sound (Deep Cove) without the cruise is possible via Real Journeys for US $62 pp each way, and accommodation at the Deep Cove Hostel can be arranged for casual visitors (from US $19/night).

The area is well worth a several-night stay – it's remote, comfortable, and far less crowded than Milford.

There are short walks around Helena Falls and along the Olivia River (Old Doubtful Sound Track), as well as up to Hanging Valley.

Small dinghies can be hired by the half day from the hostel for fishing, or you can travel with your own pack-raft

Milford Road Conditions

The Milford Road is one of the most dangerous roads in New Zealand, primarily because of its narrow and winding nature, the volume of traffic it sees in high season, the number of international drivers, and the distracting scenery.

It's not uncommon to see tourists only half pulled off the road for photo opportunities, or crawling along at too-slow speeds, creating pressure and incentive for high-risk passing.

Be smart, drive sensibly, always pull completely off the road if you're stopping, and use pullouts to let others pass if you're not in a hurry.

Lake Manapouri
Douglas Thom

or inflatable SUP – both of which can be hired in Te Anau.

Hiking around Lake Manapouri

The Lake Manapouri region also provides heaps of adventure opportunities for those of you on a budget. Bush tracks exist a short boat ride – or a swim for the brave – across the Waiau River outlet.

The Circle Track loops its way to a great view over bush-covered hills, and the Hope Arm Track leads to either the tiny (free) two-bunk Back Valley hut (and other three wire bridge) or the Hope Arm hut, where pristine beach camping is also available.

Hope Arm is also the launching point for most ascents of Mt. Titaroa, the iconic granite sloped peak visible to the south of Te Anau. It's a non-technical ascent, and well worth a couple days' effort.

The lake is ideal for paddling. Unfortunately, there are no self-hire kayaking options in Fiordland, but, stand up paddleboards and pack-rafts can be hired in nearby Te Anau.

There are amazing and unspoilt sandy

coves near Stoney Point, and a trip up The Monument near Hope Arm (boat travel required) is guaranteed to be a highlight for those who aren't put off by vertigo-inducing drops.

Hike the Dusky Track

The West Arm, which is passed through on any trip to Doubtful Sound, is the launching point for the infamous Dusky Track, as well as Fiordland's best (and only) mountain bike ride, Percy Pass. Both of these options are typically one-way affairs requiring transport logistics, so make sure to get more information before setting out.

Fiordland is such a vast and magical place that these ideas really just scratch the surface of what the region has to offer for those of you looking to get off the beaten path. Whatever you do, you're sure to be impressed.

Namu: The Sandfly

There is a Maori legend that 'Namu' (the sandfly) was created and released near Milford Sound to keep people from lingering too long in this beautiful place and spoiling it. In many ways, it appears to be working!

For many tourists, an encounter with the sandfly is the worst thing about their trip. A few tips on how to deal with the pesky critters can go a long way to making the scenery be the main thing that stands out in your experience:

1. **Move:** Sandflies can't keep up for long if you're moving. So, if they're abundant, strolling along will keep most of them at bay.

2. **Cover up:** If you're keen to stop and relax, cover up. Shorts might seem like a great idea on a hot day, but less so when your legs are covered in sandflies. The insects can't bite through anything, so lightweight nylon trousers and sleeves are a good idea. A head-net for those camping on beaches that want to enjoy sunrise/sunset – when they are most vicious – is also a good idea.

3. **Use repellant:** DEET and similar sprays will work temporarily, but require frequent reapplication to be effective.

Stewart Island

Hailed for a real sense of isolation, Stewart Island is an ideal destination for nature lovers and adventure seekers, tucked away at the southernmost end of the country.

Wohlers lookout, Stewart Island

Cage diving with sharks

Protected in New Zealand waters, Great White Sharks are frequent between the stretch of water separating Stewart Island from the South Island.

Get up close and personal with these predators by taking a tour out into the heart of shark territory, and get dropped into a cage underwater to come face to face with the oceans' second deadliest creature (contrary to popular belief, Killer Whales are the apex predator).

Hiking trails

Stewart Island has numerous hiking trails, but the flagship track is through

Rakiura National Park, Stewart Island

Rakiura National Park. It's a 20mi (32km) loop along the coastline, through dense forests and past historical sites.

Kiwi spotting and bird watching

Stewart Island is the only place in New Zealand where Kiwi birds outnumber human residents – the human population is around 400. You might hear these nocturnal birds calling at night, but join a Kiwi spotting adventure with a local guide to try see one in the flesh.

Stewart Island is a healthy habitat for our winged friends. Expect to share most of your moments with the curious Kaka, and listen out for the Bellbird, Tui, and Grey Warbler among other species native to the region.

Scuba diving

Stewart Island enjoys a diverse marine

> Stewart Island is the only place in New Zealand where Kiwi birds outnumber human residents.

Horseshoe Bay, Stewart Island

ecosystem, thanks to a warm current from the Australian Great Barrier Reef. Temperatures range between 46–57°F (8–14°C), but visibility is outstanding and marine species thrive. The Paterson Inlet Marine Reserve has 170 species of seaweed and over 50 species of fish.

Ulva Island

One of New Zealand's few predator-free sanctuaries, Ulva Island, is a 269-hectare island in the Paterson Inlet. Native bird species include the Stewart Island Brown Kiwi, South Island Saddleback, and the Stewart Island Robin.

Sunset kayaking

Kayak along Stewart Island's peaceful and pristine bays at dusk. The island's southerly position means late, lingering sunsets in summer.

Rakiura Museum

Visit New Zealand's smallest museum, run entirely by volunteers. The Rakiura museum offers a unique insight into the history of Stewart Island, the early whaling community, mutton birding, and Maori history.

Watch "A Local's Tail"

Hear and watch the history of Stewart Island through a quirky (and dated) 40-minute film, narrated by a dog on screen. It's light watching, but a fun and cheesy insight into the island in a tiny theatre.

Local delicacies

The most famous local delicacy is muttonbird, or *tītī*. Stewart Island Maori have rights to gather muttonbird on 36 nearby islands, between April 1st and May 31st each year. The meat has a slightly salty taste to it, due to the bird's fish diet and habitat.

Another New Zealand local seafood is *paua*, which has a brightly-colored blue and green shell. Try them both at Church Hill, which only serves locally-produced food.

Know Before You Go

• You won't find shopping malls or a raging nightlife on Stewart Island, so be prepared for a relaxed stay.

• The local Four Square is well-stocked, but you can bring food over from the South Island.

• Weather can be unpredictable, with rainy days common in the middle of summer, so pack for all conditions.

• Get to Stewart Island by a 20-minute flight from Invercargill or one-hour ferry from Bluff. A flight will cost a little more than the ferry. It's worth checking out flights into Dunedin as well as Invercargill to see what is cheaper. Be aware you'll still have to drive about three hours to Bluff from Dunedin.

• Accommodation books out quickly during peak season (Dec–Feb). There are several lodges and one pub-hotel in the sole township of Oban, but a *bach* or *crib* (local terms for a modest holiday home or beach house) may be more affordable.

Abel Tasman and Nelson Lakes

Every year, visitors flock to Abel Tasman National Park for golden sand beaches, energetic birdlife, and coastal views. Just a few hours inland, you'll find Nelson Lakes National Park – a massive sprawl of snowy peaks, icy waterfalls, and roaring rivers.

Lake Rotoiti, Nelson Lakes

For easy exploring in the sunshine, head to Abel Tasman. For adventure, Nelson Lakes. Or, why not make time for both?

Abel Tasman National Park

The 37mi (60km) Abel Tasman Coastal Track forms the centerpiece of this National Park. It's a three-to-five days' hike along the warm golden coastline, and one of the island's most scenic easy hikes. Even better, a water taxi can drop you off and pick you up, so you can easily experience just a day or two on the trail. Bark Bay to Anchorage is a particularly spectacular section – if it's low tide, take your shoes and socks off and enjoy the shortcut across the wide tidal flats.

Abel Tasman is a great place for easy exploring, but because of that you'll be competing with huge summer crowds. For something more adventurous and less trafficked, head inland.

Nelson Lakes National Park

Just an hour away from Able Tasman,

> 66
> Abel Tasman is a great place for easy exploring, but because of that you'll be competing with huge summer crowds.

you'll find St Arnaud, your base for adventures in Nelson Lakes National Park. From here, water taxis can transport you across the region's lakes for short walks and nights spent stargazing.

To get further inland, you'll need to go on foot. And to access the gem of the park – Blue Lake, home to the clearest water in the world – you'll need a few days up your sleeve.

Day trips

Take a water taxi up Lake Rotoroa to Sabine or D'Urville Hut. Head out for the day, walk the trails for a few hours, and take a boat back out. A water taxi can also take you up Lake Rotoiti to Lakehead Hut, where you can enjoy the flat, two-hour walk back out along the lakeside.

In St Arnaud, walk the tracks around town looking for rare birds, and keep an

Kayaking in the Abel Tasman

Angelus, among yellow alpine tussock.

Even though it's just an overnight trip, pack for all seasons. Travelers have reported snowfall in mid-summer (January). The hut is manned over summer by volunteer hut wardens who can update you on weather, track conditions, and the best way down the mountain if bad weather comes in.

Take the Travers–Sabine circuit

The Travers-Sabine track shows off the very best of the park. It's a four-to-seven day walk, covering 50mi (80km), but it's a good idea to allow yourself the full seven days for this adventure.

Venture up the Travers Valley, past thundering waterfalls and across a few rivers to Travers Hut in the upper reaches of the valley, among rocky peaks and icy rivers. If you've got good weather, follow the track up and over the misty Travers Saddle to West Sabine Hut the following day.

Leave your pack at the hut and take a day to explore Blue Lake, about two hours up the valley from West Sabine Hut. This is the jewel of the area – a small blue lake that's been officially crowned the world's clearest water. Your last two days are spent walking out via the deep green Sabine Valley – leave some time for lake swims.

Sure, a huge amount of effort is needed to fully explore this park, but that's why the area is so spectacular. The Travers Valley, Sabine Valley, and Blue Lake are some of New Zealand's most spectacular sights, and you could easily experience them in mid-summer without another person in sight.

eye out for the famous multi-colored Mandarin Duck that might be on the lakefront.

Overnight trip to Lakehead

For an overnight trip, take a boat into Lakehead or Sabine Hut, and take a boat or hike out the next day. You'll need to take sleeping bags and food with you, but the huts have mattresses and fireplaces.

Lakehead Hut sits on the edge of an open grassy expanse at the head of Lake Rotoiti, so it's an amazing spot for stargazing on clear evenings.

Robert Ridge to Angelus Hut

Pack your bags and head up Robert Ridge to Angelus Hut for a night (six hours, 7.6mi/12.2km, intermediate). This range rises between the two lakes, with amazing views of the surrounding area. The hut is located on the edge of Lake

> "
> Sure, a huge amount of effort is needed to fully explore this park, but that's why the area is so spectacular.

ADVENTURE

Adventure and New Zealand have become synonymous, and with good reason: There's no shortage of crazy activities to get your heart racing and test even the most fearless of travelers. Would you expect anything less from the country that invented bungee jumping?

North Island Adventure

Auckland

You don't have to go far from the international terminal once you've landed in Auckland for a unique thrill. Get epic views of New Zealand's biggest city by walking outside the top of the iconic Sky Tower and hang off the edge, or if you're up to it, base jump off the top with a wire on your back.

Northland

As you head north of Auckland, you have hundreds of miles of wilderness right at your fingertips. Try scuba diving at Poor Knights Island, which is considered some of the best in New Zealand.

Other options include canyoning at Piha in steep volcanic valleys, paragliding over 90 Mile Beach, or swimming with wild dolphins in the Bay of Islands: take your pick.

If you only do one thing, there's no adventure quite so thrilling as sandboarding at Te Paki Sand Dunes near Cape Reinga. Hold on tight to your boogie board, because you're not stopping 'til you hit the bottom.

Western North Island

Everyone knows the seaside town of Raglan for its epic left hand break. A great place to hang out, chill, and learn to surf, few travelers dig deep enough to know there are plenty of other ways to get the blood pumping, like canyoning, caving, and climbing.

Cathedral Cove Bay

> Summer is best for exploring the furthest reaches of the country, including the uninhabited highlands which are inaccessible for the rest of the year.

The most famous glow-worm caves in New Zealand are in the rural area of Waitomo, and the best way to experience them is to abseil into them on a black water rafting tour, where you cave, climb, zip line, and raft underground.

Head south and do a multi-day paddle of the Whanganui River, a place so important it was the first river in the world to be given legal status as a person.

One of the best adventures on the North Island is to climb the perfect volcanic peak of Mt. Taranaki. Normally a one-day return trip, in summer you can often see clear halfway across the North Island.

Coromandel

The Coromandel Peninsula is a stunning part of the North Island, with rugged terrain and a beautiful coastline.

Tongariro
Liz Carlson

Skip walking and head out to Cathedral Cove by kayak or even sign up to go diving there. Jump and abseil your way through the stunning canyons, and build in some time for the hikes and day walks in the area. You can even explore the Coromandel riding on horseback with locals.

Central North Island

Rotorua, nicknamed Roto-Vegas by locals, is home to almost any adventure you could imagine. From zip lining through a native forest to zooming down the world's highest commercially-rafted waterfall, you can do it all in a day. There are plenty of hidden hot pools and geothermal parks work exploring. Be sure to grab a mountain bike and hit up some of New Zealand's most famous downhill trails and jumps on the Skyline or in the Redwoods Forest.

An adventure around the North Island would be incomplete without hiking the famous Tongariro Crossing.

Nearby in Taupo, you can opt to touch the water on their famous bungee jump or chuck yourself out of a plane, strapped to a stranger, over the biggest lake in New Zealand.

An adventure around the North Island would be incomplete without hiking the famous Tongariro Crossing, a day walk which weaves its way near three stunning volcanoes: Tongariro, Ruapehu, and Ngauruhoe – which you might recognize from *The Lord of the Rings*.

In winter, there are two local ski resorts on Ruapehu that serve up some of the best skiing on the North Island.

Bay of Plenty

The Bay of Plenty is home to some great surfing and seaside activities, like swimming with wild dolphins. You can skydive here, or boat/helicopter

Liz Carlson

Rotorua

The Wairarapa

The lovely region where Wellingtonians escape to wine and dine on the weekends is also home to some unique and local adventures, like a sunrise hot air balloon flight or a walk to the weirdly-formed Putangirua Pinnacles.

With the Tararuas on your doorstep, there are plenty of hikes through these wild and challenging mountains. Check out some of the local backcountry huts here on a multi-day adventure, but be sure you know what you're doing.

Wellington

New Zealand's coolest little capital of Wellington is home to far more trendy bars and hipster cafes than tourist adventures. But its location right on the water, with the top of the South Island looming in the distance, makes it an adventurer's playground.

From catching waves in Lyall Bay to grabbing your SUP board and hitting one of the many peaceful beaches, adventures in Wellington generally mean being by the sea.

out to White Island and hike around an actively erupting volcano – hardhats are included, just in case.

You can kayak to see glow-worms after dark nearby, though perhaps one of the most unique adventure activities in all of New Zealand is blokarting. Invented in the Bay of Plenty by locals, you can race a land style go-kart with a sail around the race track.

Hawke's Bay

While Hawke's Bay is best known for its wine scene, there are plenty of adventure activities that don't involve Merlot.

Whether it's mountain biking, horseback riding, hiking, or white water rafting, adventure is everywhere here if you know where to look. If you have a few thousand dollars to spare, you can even go for a joyride in a fighter jet.

> 66
> With the Tararuas on your doorstep, there are plenty of hikes through these wild and challenging mountains.

Putangirua Pinnacles

South Island Adventure

West Coast

The West Coast is the place for glacier adventures. Hike through stunning scenery to reach glacier viewpoints in Westland Tai Poutini National Park, or hop in a helicopter to get up close to Franz Josef and Fox glaciers.

Guided heli-hiking expeditions, which drop people off where the ice is stable enough to go for a hike, are also available.

Raging white-water is another reason to linger, and rivers range from moderate to extreme. Or, go for a guided spelunking adventure, complete with squeezing through tight cracks and rappelling in the Te Tahi cave system.

Nelson and Marlborough

This region offers plenty of adventures aside from the Abel Tasman and Queen Charlotte hiking trails. Raft or kayak the Buller River, try out quad biking nearby, go snorkeling, scuba diving, take a sailing lesson, rock climb,

Fox Glacier

Otago

> " The West Coast is the place for glacier adventures. Hike through stunning scenery to reach glacier viewpoints in Westland Tai Poutini National Park.

or try tandem paragliding.

Or, opt for a ride on the Skywire, a four-seat cable car that soars through the forest at up to 62mi/hour (100 km/hour).

Otago

Otago peninsula is one of the best places to watch penguins, and catch a glimpse of other wildlife like seals, sea lions, and royal albatross.

Explore the Sandfly Bay Track, enjoy the beaches, take a scuba or snorkeling lesson, go horseback riding, fly-fishing, or mountain biking.

For a less strenuous activity, stroll around Larnach Castle or ride the Taieri Gorge Railway for spectacular scenery.

Dunedin

Home to the University of Otago, Dunedin is well-known for its rugby, scenery, and coast, and it's a great place to take a surfing lesson or try mountain biking.

See the Moeraki Boulders about 43mi (70km) north of town, where you can see the famous smooth boulders – a photographer's paradise!

Southland

Take the Stewart Island Ferry across the raging waters of Foveaux Strait to Stewart Island, and explore Rakiura National Park by hiking the Rakiura Great Walk.

Hop on a water taxi to Ulva Island to take a hike – be sure to keep an eye out for the elusive kiwi. Kayak trips are available, as well as mountain biking and horse trekking.

Fiordland

Kayak or take a cruise to explore Milford Sound's stunning waterfalls. Milford Road is lined with great hikes, but if you're looking for a longer adventure, try the world-famous Milford, Kepler, or Hollyford tracks.

To see glow worms in Te Anau, cruise across the lake to explore the cave by foot or via a short boat ride. It's an otherworldly experience to glide through the pitch-black caves, lit only by thousands of glow worms dotting the walls.

Queenstown

New Zealand's adventure capital offers an endless number of adrenaline-charged activities. Select from a number of scenic bungee jumps, ride a jetboat on the Shotover River, go white-water rafting, or try a boat-towed paraflight.

Paragliding over Queenstown

Pariwaz Billimoria

> New Zealand's adventure capital offers an endless number of adrenaline-charged activities.

Hydro Attack offers a unique, "shark like" aquatic ride in a submersible that dives, leaps, and moves at up to 49mi/ hour (80km/hour). Levitate above Lake Wakatipu with a water-jet powered "Flyboard" or take an aqua bike, pedal boat, kayak, or paddleboard for a spin.

The options are endless, including canyoning, river surfing, zip lining, mountain biking, and rock climbing. In winter, skiers and snowboarders flock to Coronet Peak and The Remarkables.

Wanaka

Hike Mount Aspiring National Park, go canyoning, rock climbing, mountaineering, skydiving, parasailing, biking, kayaking, rafting, or jetboating. Shop around town to find the best tour operator and price for your budget.

In winter, skiers and snowboarders head to nearby Treble Cone Ski Area and Cardrona Alpine Resort. Cross-country skiers go to Snow Farm, with 34mi (55km) of trails – that are also open for tramping and mountain biking in summer.

Hiking on the North Island

Tongariro Alpine Crossing

Often classed as one of the best day hikes in the world, you'll be challenged by the 'devil's staircase' and slippery scree slopes on the Tongariro Alpine Crossing, but rewarded with incredible turquoise sulphur lakes and a volcanic moonscape. Weather can be very temperamental, so come prepared with waterproofs and layers.

- **Distance:** 12.5mi (20km)
- **Time needed:** one full day
- **Difficulty:** moderate

Approaching Rangitoto Summit

Rangitoto Summit

Rangitoto is an unmissable sight from Auckland — it's the volcanic island that rises out of the harbor. Hiking to the summit is an easy amble through native pohutukawa forest. At the top, you're treated to stunning panoramic views of the harbor and Auckland city, where you'll understand why it's called the 'city of sails'.

- **Distance:** 1.8mi (3 km)

Coromandel Coast

- **Time needed:** three-to-four hours/half a day
- **Difficulty:** easy

Cape Brett Walkway

Located in beautiful Northland, the Cape Brett Walkway follows a cliff-side path and passes through native bush. The coastal views are amazing, and you'll also get the chance to stop at Deep Water Cove for some swimming, snorkeling, and beach time. It's recommended to stay at the Cape Brett Hut overnight (bookings required).

- **Distance:** 9.9mi (16km) each way
- **Time needed:** two days
- **Difficulty:** moderate

Coromandel Coastal Walk

The Coromandel Peninsula is a gorgeous area of beaches, thermal activity, native forests, and rugged coastline. Experience all of these on the quiet and

> " Rangitoto is an unmissable sight from Auckland — it's the volcanic island that rises out of the harbor.

Elen Turner
Coromandel

remote Coromandel Coastal Walk. It's also possible to mountain bike this one.
- **Distance:** 6.2mi (10km)
- **Time needed:** seven hours/a full day
- **Difficulty:** easy

Putangirua Pinnacles

Located near Wellington are these enormous gravel pillars, which are unlike anything else in the country, and are a wonder to walk among. Like many places in New Zealand, they appeared in *The Lord of the Rings* films.

Various walks can be done to and around the pinnacles along a streambed. They're located in the Aorangi Forest Park.
- **Distance:** 4.4mi (7km)
- **Time needed:** three hours/half a day
- **Difficulty:** easy

Lake Waikaremoana

The eastern part of the North Island is sparsely-populated and rarely-visited by tourists, which makes this the perfect wilderness destination.

Lake Waikaremoana is surrounded by bush-covered hills and inlets. Hikers can trek the entire perimeter in three-to-

four days, or embark on much shorter trips of half a day or less, to points of interest like waterfalls, cliffs, and lookout points.
- **Distance:** various
- **Time needed:** one hour to four days
- **Difficulty:** easy to moderate

Te Araroa

The Te Araroa trail will appeal if you want to string a whole heap of day-hikes together for one mega-adventure. This 1,864mi (3,000km) trail starts at Cape Reinga in the Far North, and extends all the way down to Bluff at the bottom of the South Island.

It's possible to just trek the North Island parts of Te Araroa. The landscape of the North Island is extremely diverse, from the semi-sub-tropical beaches of Northland to the plains of Waikato, the dense forest of the King Country, and the volcanic plateau of the Central North Island – tackling the top half of Te Araroa allows you to see it all.
- **Distance:** 683.5mi (1,100km) for the North Island section
- **Time needed:** several months
- **Difficulty:** challenging

Tips for Responsible Tramping

- Carry your rubbish out with you.
- Strictly follow 'no dogs allowed' rules if they exist, to avoid endangering native and rare wildlife.
- Only light fires where you're permitted to do so.
- Don't free-camp unless it's allowed; huts provide accommodation in many national park areas.

Hiking on the South Island

The Routeburn track

The Routeburn traverses from the upper end of Lake Wakatipu (near Queenstown) to The Divide, halfway along the road from Te Anau to Milford Sound.

With its big mountain scenery, cascading waterfalls, and perfect alpine plunge pools, there's no wonder why this is one of New Zealand's "Great Walks".

- **Distance:** 20mi (32km)
- **Time needed:** three days
- **Difficulty:** intermediate

DOC huts on the Routeburn track

The Milford track

The Milford track runs from the top end of Lake Te Anau to the back entrance into Milford Sound. You start on a boat. You end on a boat.

For isolation, the Milford Track is unrivalled among New Zealand's popular tramps – this is helped by the fact that only 100 people can walk the track per day.

The track climbs over MacKinnon Pass (don't miss New Zealand's tallest waterfall, or New Zealand's most scenic toilet) and into the Arthur Valley. Bonus points if it's raining on your last day on the track: hundreds of waterfalls cascade down the sides of the valley, and emerging into Milford Sound in the mist is spectacular.

- **Distance:** 33.5mi (54km)
- **Time needed:** four days
- **Difficulty:** intermediate

The Kepler track

The Kepler, at the south end of Lake Te Anau, is the area's slightly lesser-known cousin, but still a "Great Walk". After a steep one-day climb to Luxmore Hut, you'll traverse a mountainous backbone between sharp peaks before walking out alongside waterfalls and winding rivers.

The tramping season runs from October–April, and to walk any of these three tracks, you'll need to book bunks in the huts, or campsites. They're not cheap (US $45–50 per night for huts, US $10-15 for campsites), but well worth the money if you've got the budget to do it.

Extra costs include transport (buses are your most affordable option). Te Anau is your best base for the Milford and Kepler tracks, Queenstown is an option if you're doing the Routeburn.

- **Distance:** 37mi (60km)

> With its big mountain scenery, cascading waterfalls, and perfect alpine plunge pools, there's no wonder why this is one of New Zealand's "Great Walks".

Hiking in Fiordland National Park

> The Gillespie Pass track sits above the northern tip of Lake Wanaka. You'll clamber up mountain valleys and over high passes, with snowy peaks all around.

- **Time needed:** three-to-four days
- **Difficulty:** intermediate

The Greestone-Caples

The Greenstone-Caples is a loop track just a few valleys south of the Routeburn Track. You'll wander up along the Greenstone River – meandering open valley at times, thundering narrow gorge in others – and over McKellar Saddle, a low crossing among snowy mountains.

You walk out along the Caples valley, where you should keep an eye out for bright blue glacial swimming holes. As well as mountain views, you'll see calm lakes and gnarled goblin forests.
- **Distance:** 38mi (61km)
- **Time needed:** four days
- **Difficulty:** easy to intermediate

The Rees-Dart track

Huge mountains sit behind Glenorchy, near Queenstown, and this track cuts through them. You'll cross grassy valleys, sidle around alpine basins, and climb up onto the Rees Saddle to incredible views – think massive glaciers clinging to steep mountain faces.

Plan for an extra day to take a side trip up Cascade Saddle, but only attempt it if it's dry and clear, this route can be slippery and dangerous if it's wet or snowing.
- **Distance:** 43mi (69km)
- **Time needed:** four-to-six days
- **Difficulty:** advanced

Gillespie Pass

The Gillespie Pass track sits above the northern tip of Lake Wanaka. You'll clamber up mountain valleys and over high passes, with snowy peaks all around. Leave time for a side trip to Crucible Lake when you reach Siberia Hut.
- **Distance:** 36mi (58km)
- **Time needed:** three-to-four days
- **Difficulty:** advanced

52

Essential Insurance Tips

Whether you're bungee jumping in Christchurch or skiing in Queenstown, ind out how and if travel insurance policies can cover you. And, because New Zealand is the home of extreme sports, there are a few risky activities that we can't cover you for, so we'll go over them too.

Bungee Jumping

As New Zealand is the commercial home to bungee, a lot of travelers visit knowing they're going to try it. Travelers from all countries of residence, except Brazil (our Brazilian insurer doesn't allow us), can be covered for bungee jumping. And, because we work with different insurers around the world, no policy is the same.

Most policies automatically cover bungee jumping, but there are a few that require you to add it on to your policy when you buy it. This also means an additional premium. So make sure you check before you buy. If you've selected the right policy and you're injured while bungee jumping, the policy covers overseas medical expenses including: hospitalization, out-patient treatment and medical transport to the most appropriate hospital. If you're seriously injured and

need to be flown home for ongoing treatment, the policy covers that too. But, as it's travel insurance, once you're home, cover stops, so you'll need access to private medical insurance or government healthcare to cover your ongoing costs.

Skiing and Snowboarding

New Zealand's slopes provide ample opportunity to hone your skills. Big dumps, fresh tracks, and bluebird days will make for an epic trip, yet accidents on and off the hill do happen – even to the most experienced sliders. Unlike bungee jumping, all of our insurers cover skiing and ski boarding, though not all policies do, so it's up to you to select the correct policy at the time of purchase.

When you get a quote online, you'll see that there's a list of sports and activities with the corresponding level of cover next to it. It's important to read through that list so you know if you need to upgrade your policy. It's worth remembering that you can't upgrade a policy once it's been purchased. So, if you buy a policy without the correct cover for skiing or snowboarding, you'll need to buy an additional policy for the time you're on the slopes in New Zealand (or anywhere else for that matter!). And as you've traveled on your policy, you won't be able to get a refund.

If you've selected and bought the correct policy, you're not putting yourself needlessly at risk, and you're adhering to the policy terms and conditions, if you tear an ACL

> Big dumps, fresh tracks, and bluebird days will make for an epic trip, yet accidents on and off the hill do happen – even to the most experienced sliders.

or MCL, pop a knee, or are involved in any other injury as a result of skiing or snowboarding, the policy covers medivac including ski patrol, hospitalization, out-patient treatment, and other medical expenses. You can read more about <u>here</u>.

What's Not Covered by Travel Insurance?

While seeing New Zealand from the air might be appealing, if you find yourself paragliding and you're not an American, British, or Irish resident, you won't be covered. And even then, you have to select the correct policy to go paragliding. It is a risky sport, and most of our insurers have made the decision not to cover it.

There are also general exclusions and limits to how you're covered. If you expose yourself to a needless risk and do something ridiculous, – like trying to ski a black run when you're a beginner, going bungee jumping with an unlicensed provider, or participating in any activity which your policy doesn't cover – then we're not able to help you with any financial assistance.

Milford Sound

Pariraz Bilmoria

54

Notes

Notes

Notes

Notes

Notes

Notes

Notes

Notes

Notes

Notes

Notes

Notes

Notes

Notes

Notes

Notes

Notes

Notes

Printed in Great Britain
by Amazon